MLB TEAMS

Philadelphia PHILLIES

KENNY ABDO

Fly!
An Imprint of Abdo Zoom
abdobooks.com

abdobooks.com

Published by Abdo Zoom, a division of ABDO, P.O. Box 398166, Minneapolis, Minnesota 55439.

Printed in the United States of America, North Mankato, Minnesota.
102025
012026

Photo Credits: Getty Images, Granger Collection, Shutterstock
Production Contributors: Kenny Abdo, Jennie Forsberg, Grace Hansen
Design Contributors: Candice Keimig, Neil Klinepier

Library of Congress Control Number: 2025936786

Publisher's Cataloging-in-Publication Data

Names: Abdo, Kenny, author.
Title: Philadelphia Phillies / by Kenny Abdo
Description: Minneapolis, Minnesota : Abdo Zoom, 2026 | Series: MLB teams | Includes online resources and index.
Identifiers: ISBN 9798384940289 (lib. bdg.) | ISBN 9798384941040 (ebook) | ISBN 9798384941422 (read-to-me ebook)
Subjects: LCSH: Philadelphia Phillies (Baseball team)--Juvenile literature. | Baseball teams--Juvenile literature. | Professional sports--Juvenile literature. | Sports franchises--Juvenile literature. | Major League Baseball (Organization)--Juvenile literature.
Classification: DDC 796.357--dc23

Table of CONTENTS

PHILLIES

For nearly 150 years, the Philadelphia Phillies have turned big hits into big wins. Like the Liberty Bell, the team remains a true Philly symbol despite a crack or two.

Even with the rough moments in its history, the team that hails from the City of Brotherly Love has still managed to stay in the hearts of its fans.

TOYOTA
Choose Blue.
WHO BUT
W.B.MASON
SINCE 1898
Budweiser
Ninety Nine
Jefferson
10
387

BATTER UP!

The Philadelphia Phillies debuted in 1883. They are the oldest team in Major League Baseball to keep the same name and city. The 1894 team's batting average was .349, a single-season **record** that still stands. Tuck Turner had the highest average of the team with .418.

In 1915, the Phillies won their first **National League (NL) pennant**. Star pitcher Grover Cleveland Alexander led the team with 31 wins. The team reached the World Series but lost to the Red Sox in five games.

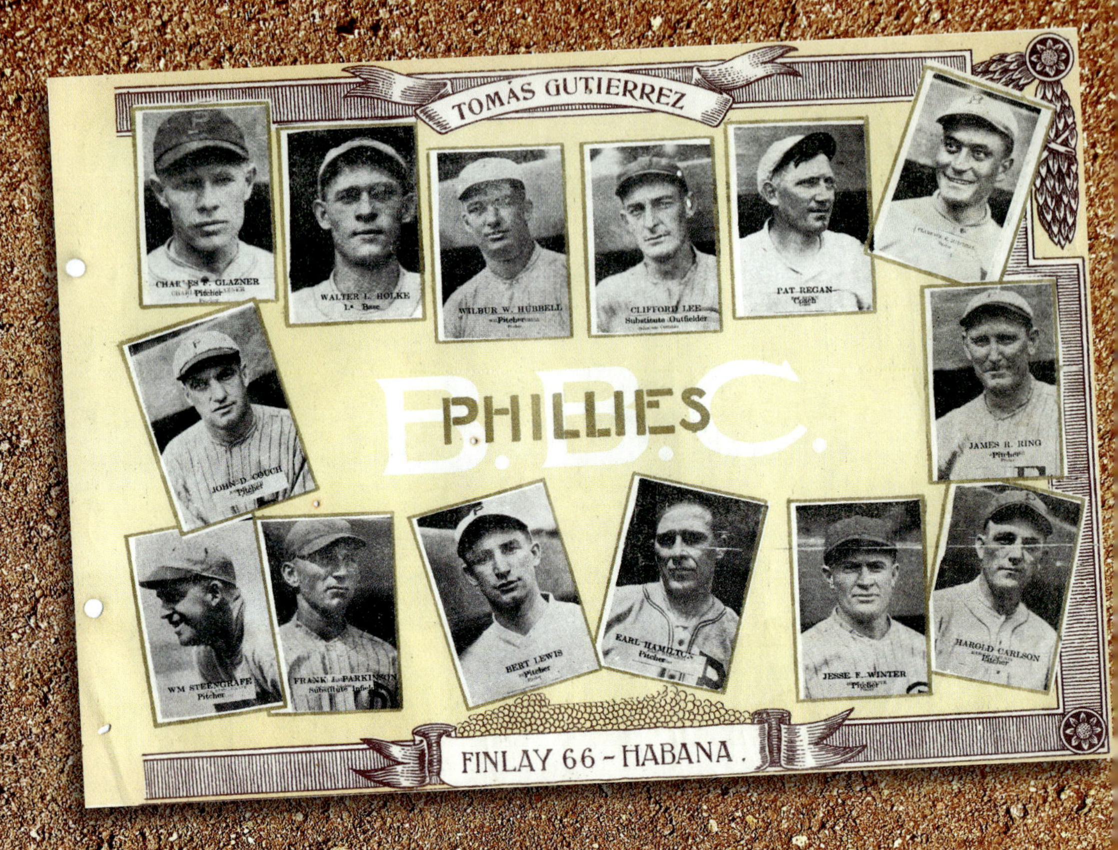

From 1918 to 1948, the Phillies had just one winning season. Still, outfielder Chuck Klein stood out. He won the MVP Award in 1932 and led the league in home runs four times. In 1933, Klein earned the **Triple Crown** by leading in batting average, home runs, and **RBIs**.

GRAND SLAMS

In 1950, the young core of Phillies players known as "the Whiz Kids" helped the team win the **NL pennant**. The young stars, such as power threat Del Ennis, pitcher Robin Roberts, and shortstop Granny Hamner, took the Phillies all the way to the World Series.

CHMIDT
20

The Phillies started out slow in 1980. But, with one game left in the season, Mike Schmidt helped clinch the **division** title by hitting a two-run homer. Philly fought through the **NL** Championship Series to make it to the World Series. In Game 6, **closer** Tug McGraw got the final six outs to finally make the Phillies champions! Schmidt was named the World Series MVP.

Phillies
TOYOTA
Coca-Cola
MEDICINE WITH MUSCLE
W.B.MASON
Citizens Bank Park
Citizens Bank Park
State Farm
WORLD SERIES 2008

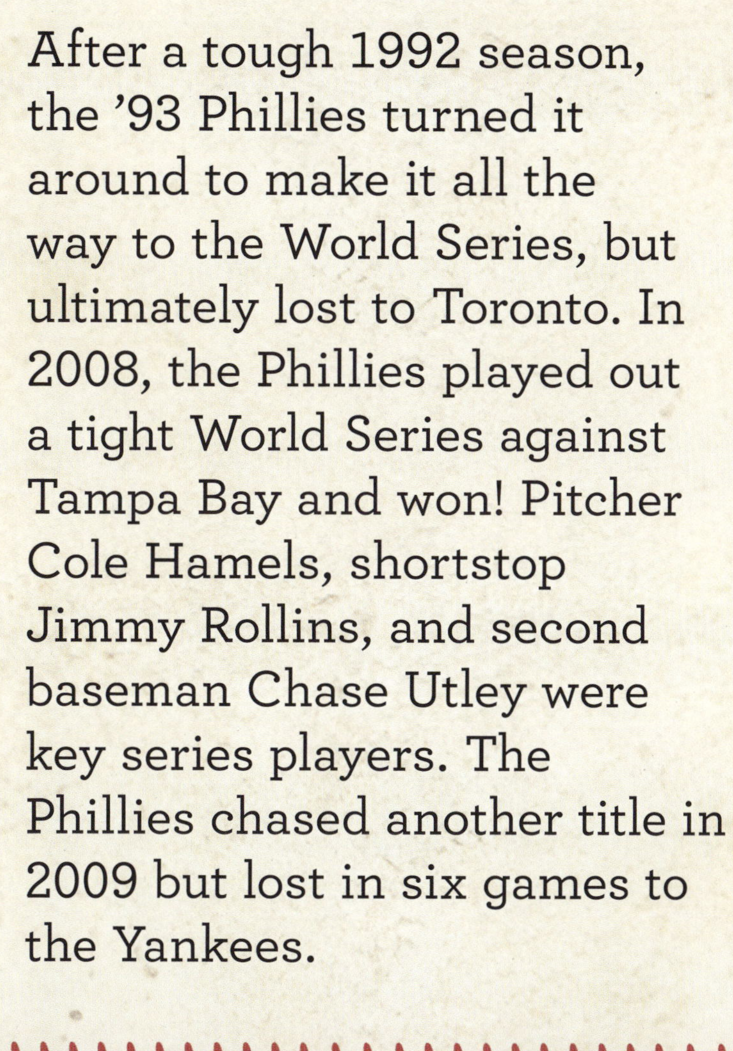

After a tough 1992 season, the '93 Phillies turned it around to make it all the way to the World Series, but ultimately lost to Toronto. In 2008, the Phillies played out a tight World Series against Tampa Bay and won! Pitcher Cole Hamels, shortstop Jimmy Rollins, and second baseman Chase Utley were key series players. The Phillies chased another title in 2009 but lost in six games to the Yankees.

In 2022, the Phillies made a surprise playoff run. Bryce Harper helped lead the team to their first **postseason** appearance and **pennant** in 11 years! Harper won the **NL** Championship Series MVP for his strong performance. Harper hit .400 with two home runs.

Harper hit 30 home runs in 2024, while Zack Wheeler posted a 2.57 **ERA**. By 2025, the Phillies had once again become one of the top teams in baseball.

Led by Wheeler and Trea Turner, the team continued to chase its third World Series title. The Phillies stay strong and the crowd stays loud, ready for the next big win.

HALL OF FAME

Mike Schmidt hit 548 home runs and won three **NL** MVP awards with the Phillies. He led the league in home runs eight times and drove in over 1,500 runs during his career. In 1980, he helped the Phillies win their first World Series and earned the Series MVP. Schmidt entered the Baseball Hall of Fame in 1995.

20

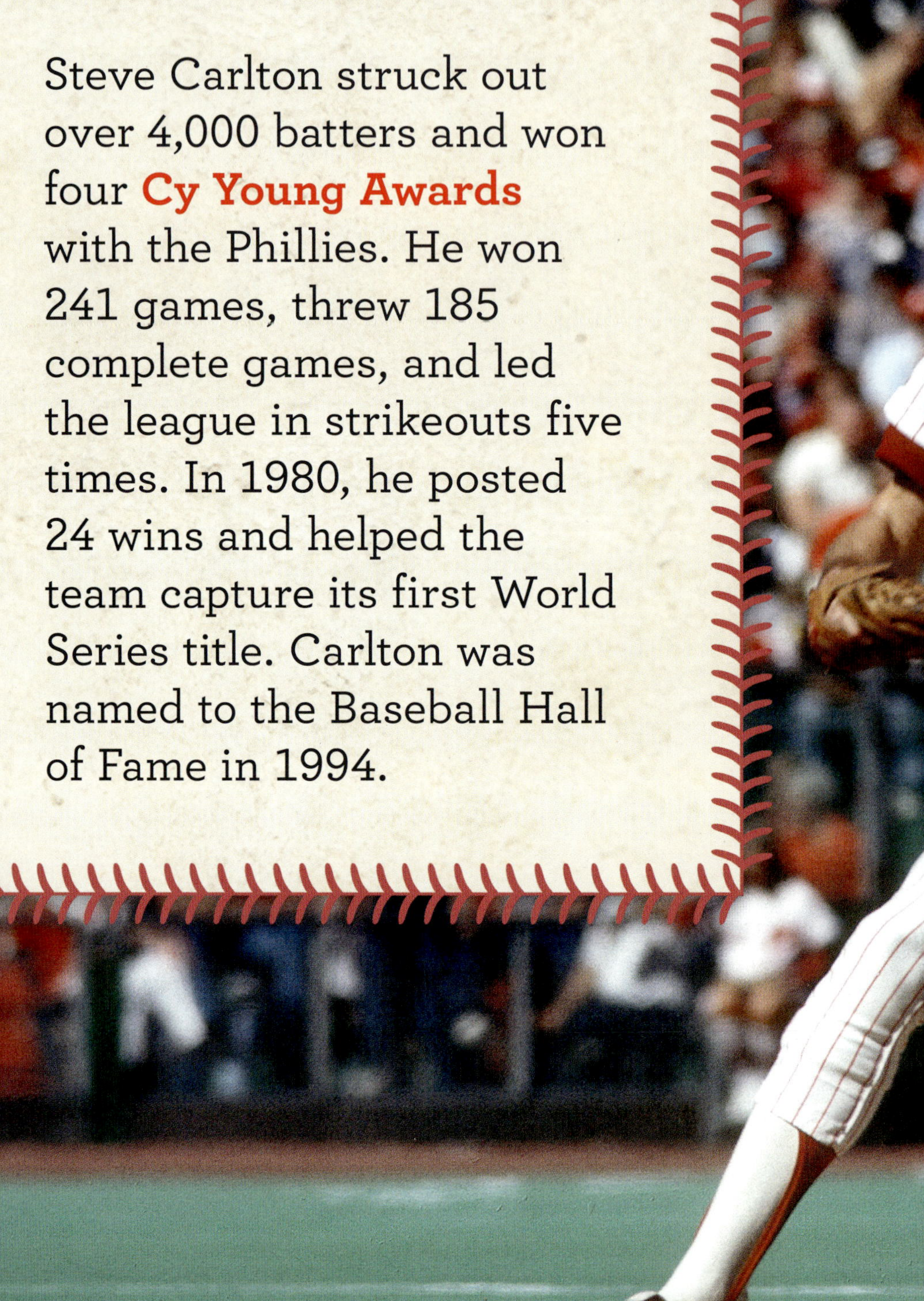

Steve Carlton struck out over 4,000 batters and won four **Cy Young Awards** with the Phillies. He won 241 games, threw 185 complete games, and led the league in strikeouts five times. In 1980, he posted 24 wins and helped the team capture its first World Series title. Carlton was named to the Baseball Hall of Fame in 1994.

P
32
P

Chase Utley hit 233 home runs and drove in 916 runs with the Phillies. He played in six **All-Star Games** and won four Silver Slugger Awards. Utley helped lead the team to the 2008 World Series title and another trip in 2009. He holds the **record** for most home runs in a single World Series by a second baseman, with five. He also stole 142 bases before leaving the team in 2015.

UTLEY
26
26

GLOSSARY

All-Star Game – a yearly baseball contest where top players from the American League (AL) and the NL compete against each other.

closer – a specialized relief pitcher who enters the game in the late innings.

Cy Young Award – an annual American baseball award given to the best pitcher in each of the two MLB leagues.

division – a number of teams grouped together in a sport for competitive purposes.

Earned-Run Average (ERA) – the average number of earned runs per game scored against a pitcher.

National League (NL) – one of two 15-team leagues that make up MLB.

pennant – the title achieved by the team that wins its division or league championship.

postseason – the playoffs, including the wild-card round, divisional playoffs, league championship series, and World Series.

record – a top achievement by a team or player that no one has done before.

Triple Crown – an achievement earned when leading the league in batting average, home runs, and RBIs in the same season.

ONLINE RESOURCES

To learn more about the Philadelphia Phillies, please visit **abdobooklinks.com** or scan this QR code. These links are routinely monitored and updated to provide the most current information available.

INDEX